Editor: Jacqueline A. Wolfe
Page Production: Tracy Kaehler
Creative Director: Keith Griffin
Editorial Director: Carol Jones

First American edition published in 2006 by
Picture Window Books
5115 Excelsior Boulevard
Suite 232
Minneapolis, MN 55416
877-845-8392
www.picturewindowbooks.com

First published by Evans Brothers Limited
2a Portman Mansions
Chiltern Street
London W1U 6NR, United Kingdom

Library of Congress Cataloging-in-Publication Data
Ganeri, Anita, 1961-
Islamic stories / by Anita Ganeri ; illustrated by Rebecca Wallis.
p. cm. — (Traditional religious tales)
Includes bibliographical references and index.
ISBN 1-4048-1313-6 (hardcover)
1. Islamic stories—Juvenile literature. I. Wallis, Rebecca, ill. II. Title.

BP87.5.G25 2006
297.1'8—dc22   2005024985

Acknowledgements
The author and publishers would like to thank the following for permission to
reproduce copyright material: page 9 Trip: page 11 Trip/Ibrahim: page 15 Trip: page
18 Trip: page 23 Trip: page 25 Trip.

ISLAMIC STORIES

by Anita Ganeri
illustrations by Rebecca Wallis

Special thanks to our advisers for their expertise:

Dany Doueiri, Ph.D.,
Chief Content Editor, http://IslamiCity.Com
USA

Susan Kesselring, M.A.,
Literacy Educator,
Rosemount-Apple Valley-Egan (Minnesota) School District

Introduction

Islamic Stories

In each of the world's six main religions—Hinduism, Judaism, Buddhism, Christianity, Islam, and Sikhism—stories play a very important role. They have been used for hundreds of years to teach people about their faith in a way that makes difficult messages easier to understand. Many stories tell of times in the lives of religious teachers, leaders, gods, and goddesses. Others explain mysterious events such as how the world was created or what happens when you die. Many have a strong moral or lesson to teach.

The collection of stories in this book comes from Islam. Islam is the religion followed by Muslims. They believe in one god, whom they call Allah. They follow Allah's guidance throughout their lives. Islam began in the 7th century B.C. in the Middle Eastern country we now call Saudi Arabia. A man called Muhammad was chosen by Allah to receive his message for the world. Muhammad was the last of all the prophets of Islam. The messages were collected together to make the Qur'an, the Muslim holy book. Allah did not speak to Muhammad directly. His messenger was an angel named Jibril (Gabriel). In this book, you can read some of the stories which show how Allah gave his message to the world through his angels and prophets.

Table of Contents

The Birth of the Prophet Muhammad

I n the year 570, the Prophet Muhammad, peace be upon him, was born in Makkah (Mecca), a city in Saudi Arabia. His father, Abdullah, died a few months before his birth. His mother's name was Amina. Amina was good and pure, and Allah, the one God, had chosen her to be Muhammad's mother.

A few days before the Prophet's birth, an angel appeared from the sky and visited Amina in her dreams.

"I bring you good news," the angel said. "Oh mother of the blessed last prophet. Your son will be the lord of the worlds, the best of men. He will save the world. When he is born, you must say these words, 'I place him under Allah's protection, safe from wickedness and envy.' And you must call him Muhammad, the praised one."

Muhammad was born just before daybreak on a Monday, on the twelfth day of the month of Rabi-ul-Awwal, in the year of the Elephant. It is said that many strange and miraculous things happened at the time

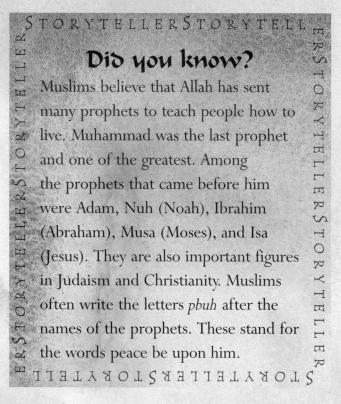

STORYTELLERStorytell
Did you know?
Muslims believe that Allah has sent many prophets to teach people how to live. Muhammad was the last prophet and one of the greatest. Among the prophets that came before him were Adam, Nuh (Noah), Ibrahim (Abraham), Musa (Moses), and Isa (Jesus). They are also important figures in Judaism and Christianity. Muslims often write the letters *pbuh* after the names of the prophets. These stand for the words peace be upon him.

of his birth. All these were signs that Allah had chosen Muhammad to be his blessed last prophet and to bring his message to the world. After his birth, Muhammad's grandfather took him to the sacred Ka'bah shrine in Makkah (Mecca) to pray to Allah and thank him for this precious gift.

As a baby, Muhammad was cared for by his foster mother, Halima, and brought up with her own son. Along with many other women, Halima had traveled to Makkah (Mecca) to look for a baby to nurse. This was the custom at that time. When she saw Muhammad, she felt sad for him. No other woman wanted to nurse him because he did not have a father. Halima was poor, but she was also kind-hearted. She took Muhammad to live in her house. And her kindness was rewarded. For while Muhammad lived with Halima, her fortunes changed, and Allah blessed her life. She had plenty of food to feed her family, her sheep and camels thrived, and her date trees blossomed.

Muhammad grew up to be healthy and strong. But when he was just 6 years old, tragedy struck. His mother, Amina, fell ill and died, leaving Muhammad an orphan. The little boy went to live with his grandfather, then with his uncle, Abu Talib, a wealthy merchant, who cared for him as his own son. He knew that his nephew was no ordinary person and that great things lay in store for him.

Muhammad grew up to be kind, thoughtful, and hardworking, and he was loved and trusted by everyone. He was known as someone who never broke his word. That is why he was called Al-Amin, which means "trusted and truthful one."

Did you know?

The city of Makkah (Mecca) in modern-day Saudi Arabia is very important for Muslims. It is the holiest city of Islam, where the Prophet Muhammad was born and where he received the words of the Qur'an, the Muslim holy book. At least once in their lifetime, all Muslims try to make a pilgrimage to Makkah (Mecca). This is called the hajj.

Did you know?

The stories in this collection come from the Qur'an, the Hadith, and the Seerat-un-Nabi. The Qur'an is the holy book of Islam. The Hadith are books of sayings and actions of the Prophet Muhammad. They show Muslims how Muhammad lived and help them to follow his example in their own lives. The Seerat-un-Nabi is the story of Muhammad's life, written by a man named Ibn Ishaq. He wrote the first biography of Muhammad. Some Muslims do not agree with the tales he tells about miracles, but his writing is mostly well respected.

The Cleansing of the Heart

According to legend, a very strange and extraordinary thing happened while Muhammad was living with Halima. One day, Muhammad was playing with his friends in the fields behind Halima's house when two angels dressed in dazzling white came walking toward him. One was carrying a silver jug, the other a golden platter piled high with snow.

The two angels grabbed hold of Muhammad's arms. One angel held him tightly, while the other took out a sharp knife. The angel cut open Muhammad's chest and took out the boy's heart. Though Muhammad could see what was happening, he did not feel any pain. Then the angel took a black speck from Muhammad's heart

Did you know?

Muslims follow five duties, called the five pillars of Islam. They support Islam, just as real pillars support a building. The first pillar is the Shahadah. This is a sentence that sums up what Muslims believe. It says: "There is no other God but Allah and Muhammad is his Prophet." The other pillars are prayer, giving alms to the poor, fasting at Ramadan, and making the pilgrimage to Makkah (Mecca).

and threw it far away. He washed the heart thoroughly in snow, to make it pure, and placed it back into the boy's body.

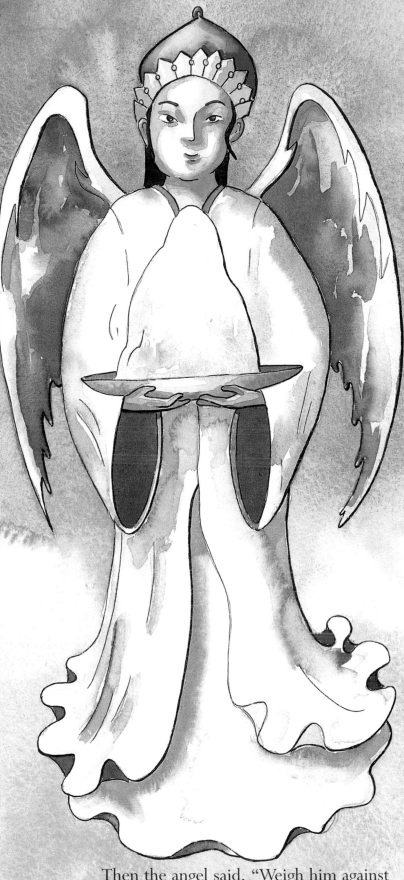

heavier, worth more than 100 others.

"Weigh him against 1,000 people," the angel said.

And they weighed him, and he was heavier, worth more than 1,000 others. Then the angels went away. When they were gone, Halima, Muhammad's foster mother, came running up to find him. His friends had told her what had happened. To her relief, she found Muhammad safe and sound, although something about him, she could not quite tell what it was, had truly changed.

STORYTELLERStoryte

Did you know?

Many Muslims believe that this story shows how Allah made Muhammad pure and clean, ready to receive his message. The black speck, which the angel took from his heart, stands for the devil's evil powers. Many other strange and wonderful events are said to have happened around the time of Muhammad's birth and childhood. They show that Muhammad was a very special person.

Then the angel said, "Weigh him against 100 people."

And they weighed him, and he was

The First Revelations

When Muhammad left Halima's house, he went to live in Makkah (Mecca), first with his grandfather, then with his uncle, Abu Talib. He worked hard as a shepherd, then as a merchant, learning his trade from Abu Talib. When he was 25 years old, he went to work for a rich and noble widow named Khadijah, who was also a merchant in Makkah (Mecca). Khadijah was not only wealthy, she was honorable, wise, and respected. She was so impressed by Muhammad's honesty and truthfulness that she sent him a proposal of marriage. Muhammad asked his uncle for his blessing. With great delight, Abu Talib agreed to the match.

For many years, Muhammad lived happily in Makkah (Mecca). He loved his wife, and his business did very well. But he also saw how much greed and cruelty there was in the world, particularly toward people who were less fortunate. Muhammad began to spend more time by himself, in prayer and meditation, trying to work out how to make things better. Sometimes he was away from home for days, staying in a cave on nearby Mount Hira, the mountain of light, and living off water, dried bread, and dates. Sometimes he heard voices saying,

"Peace be on you, Messenger of God!"

But when he looked for the speaker, there was no one there.

One day, when Muhammad was praying on Mount Hira, an amazing thing happened. A dazzling light filled the cave, and a shadowy figure of an angel appeared before him. The figure held out a piece of cloth that was covered in writing.

"Read!" the figure told Muhammad.

"I cannot read," Muhammad replied. He had never learned how to read or write.

Twice more the voice commanded him.

"Read!" the voice said.

Suddenly, Muhammad found that he could read the words and knew what they said. He felt as if the words had always been with him, written on his heart. He spoke the words out loud:

"Recite! In the name of your Lord who created all people from a clot (spot) of blood. Recite! Your Lord is the most generous one who taught people by the pen what they did not know."

Muhammad rushed from the cave and started to run down the mountainside. Then he heard a voice calling to him:

"O Muhammad, do not be afraid. You are Allah's messenger, and I am the angel Jibril (Gabriel)."

Muhammad turned and saw the mysterious figure who had spoken to him in the cave. He raced home, shaking with fear, and told Khadijah what had happened. She comforted him and reassured him, for she knew in her heart that what the angel had said was true.

Muhammad was about 40 years old. From that moment on, his life changed forever. He had been called to be Allah's prophet and to spend the rest of his life in Allah's service, teaching people how Allah wanted them to live. The way of life he taught was called Islam, which means "submitting to Allah's will." His first followers were his wife, Khadijah, his nephew, Ali, and his friend Abu Bakr, the merchant.

The Night Journey

One night, as Muhammad was sleeping near the holy mosque in Makkah (Mecca), the angel Jibril (Gabriel) came to the Prophet and woke him up. He had come to take Muhammad on an amazing journey. Jibril (Gabriel) led the Prophet to the gate of the mosque, where there stood a fabulous beast named Buraq, or Lightning. As white as snow with a horse's body, it had two great wings on its back. Jibril (Gabriel) lifted the Prophet onto Buraq's back, and together they sped through the skies to the city of Jerusalem. There Muhammad met Ibrahim (Abraham), Musa (Moses), and the other prophets who had come before him and led them in prayer.

Then Jibril (Gabriel) brought him two goblets, one full of wine and the other of milk. Muhammad drank the goblet of milk but did not touch the wine.

"You must teach your people to do the same," Jibril (Gabriel) said. "For Muslims are forbidden to drink wine."

But the Night Journey was not yet over. Up they climbed, until they reached one of the gates of heaven. There, 12,000 angels stood guard.

"Is this the true Prophet?" an angel said.

"It is," replied Jibril (Gabriel).

Together they passed through the gate and up through the seven heavens. In each of the heavens, Muhammad met the prophets who had come before him, among them Adam, Isa (Jesus), Musa (Moses), and Ibrahim (Abraham). In each of the heavens, Jibril (Gabriel) was asked:

"Who is this, O Jibril (Gabriel)?"

"Muhammad, the Prophet," Jibril (Gabriel) replied.

At last, they reached the seventh heaven, and the Prophet entered Paradise, where he came before the Throne of God, into Allah's glorious presence. There Allah gave the commandment to Muhammad that all Muslims should pray 50 times a day.

On Muhammad's way back down to Earth, he once again met Musa (Moses).

"How many times must you pray?" Musa (Moses) asked.

"Fifty times a day," said the Prophet.

"Prayer is a heavy burden," Musa (Moses) said. "And people are weak and lazy. Go back to your Lord and ask him to make the number of prayers less."

So Muhammad returned to the highest heaven and asked Allah to reduce the number of prayers. Ten prayers were taken off. But still Musa (Moses) repeated his warning, and several times more Muhammad returned to Allah and asked him to make the number of prayers less. Soon so many prayers had been taken off that only five were left. Muhammad could not go back and ask for fewer than that.

"Whoever says his prayers faithfully five times a day," Muhammad said, "shall have the same rewards as for 50."

Did you know?

In the Qur'an, heaven, or Paradise, is described as a beautiful garden where birds sing, flowers bloom, the soil smells sweet, and the rocks are made from gold and jewels. Muslims believe that people who follow Allah faithfully will go to Paradise when they die. The punishment for a wicked or sinful life is to be sent to Hell.

"Why have you killed an innocent boy?" Musa (Moses) exclaimed in horror. "That was a wicked and terrible thing to do!"

"Didn't I tell you that you would lose patience?" said the wise man again, and again Musa (Moses) apologized.

"If I ever question you again," he said, "leave me behind. I shall have deserved it."

Musa (Moses) and the wise man traveled on their way until they reached a city. They asked its people for food and shelter, but no one would help them. As they left the city, they saw a wall that was falling down, and the wise man stopped to mend it.

"Why didn't you ask for some payment in return?" asked Musa (Moses). "You could have if you'd wanted to."

"The time has come," the wise man replied, "for us to part company. But first I will explain my actions to you. The ship we saw belonged to some poor fishermen. But a king wanted to take it from them. The fishermen can easily mend the hole I bored, but it makes the ship useless to the king.

"As for the young man," the wise man continued, "his death spared his parents a lifetime of misery. They will have another son who will love them and look after them.

"As for the wall, it belonged to two city orphans whose father was a good man. Treasure is buried beneath it. It is Allah's will that, when they grow up, they will dig the treasure up. Now you know why I acted as I did. It was not my will but Allah's."

20

The Story of Ibrahim (Abraham) and Isma'il (Ishmael)

The Prophet Ibrahim (Abraham) was known as the Friend of Allah. He was humble and devout and had vowed to dedicate his life to Allah and everything dear to him. He lived peacefully with his two wives, Sara and Hajar (Hagar), and his son, Isma'il (Ishmael), whom he loved very much. The Qur'an tells the story of Ibrahim (Abraham) and Isma'il (Ishmael).

One night, Ibrahim (Abraham) had a dream. He dreamt that Allah wanted him to sacrifice his most precious possession, his beloved son, Isma'il (Ishmael). Isma'il (Ishmael) was just 10 years old, but Ibrahim (Abraham) went to find him and told him his dream.

"Father, we must do as Allah wishes," Isma'il (Ishmael) said.

So Ibrahim (Abraham) took Isma'il (Ishmael) to Mina, near the holy city of Makkah (Mecca), to carry out Allah's wishes. On the way, their path was blocked by a sinister stranger, the devil himself in disguise.

"Where are you going?" the stranger said to them.

"To carry out Allah's wishes," Ibrahim (Abraham) replied.

"But surely Allah would not wish you to kill your son," said the stranger. "That must be the work of the devil. Go home, and forget all about it."

Then Ibrahim (Abraham) recognized the stranger for whom he was and continued on his way. Next, the devil tried to tempt Isma'il (Ishmael).

"Did you know that your father is planning to kill you?" he asked the boy.

"He must do as Allah commands," Isma'il (Ishmael) replied.

A third time, the devil tried to stop them from carrying out Allah's wishes. He went to Hajar (Hagar), Isma'il's (Ishmael's) mother, but she refused to listen. Then Isma'il (Ishmael) and Ibrahim (Abraham) threw stones at the devil to drive him away.

Now it was time for the greatest test, time for Ibrahim (Abraham) to sacrifice his son. Isma'il (Ishmael) lay face down on the ground so that he could not see his father and put him off his task. Then Ibrahim (Abraham) took his knife, sharpened it, and was just about to cut Isma'il's (Ishmael's) throat, when the knife was twisted from his hand, and he heard Allah's voice calling to him:

"O Ibrahim (Abraham), do not kill your son," the voice said. "You have already shown your love and obedience to me. Sacrifice this ram instead of Isma'il (Ishmael)."

So, Ibrahim (Abraham) and Isma'il (Ishmael) caught the ram which Allah had sent and sacrificed it instead, as Allah had commanded.

STORYTELLERStory

Did you know?

Hajj begins and ends at the Ka'bah in Makkah (Mecca). This is a cube-shaped shrine that Muslims believe was built by Ibrahim (Abraham) and Isma'il (Ishmael) as a place for people to worship Allah. Every pilgrim walks around the Ka'bah seven times at the start and finish of Hajj.

STORYTELLERStoryte

Did you know?

Performing Hajj, the pilgrimage to Makkah (Mecca), is the fifth pillar of Islam. When they arrive in Makkah (Mecca), pilgrims change into simple, white clothes to show that all Muslims are equal. Then they visit various holy sites in and around Makkah (Mecca). These include a place called Mina, where they remember the story of Ibrahim (Abraham) and Isma'il (Ishmael). The pilgrims throw stones at three stone pillars that stand for the devil. They also celebrate the festival of Id-ul-Adha by sacrificing a sheep or goat.

The Story of Hajar (Hagar)

The Qur'an tells another story about Ibrahim (Abraham). Once, long ago, Allah spoke again to Ibrahim (Abraham). He told him to take Hajar (Hagar), his wife, and Isma'il (Ishmael), his young son, out to the desert and to leave them there. As always, Ibrahim (Abraham) obeyed Allah's command. He left Hajar (Hagar) and Isma'il (Ishmael) alone in the desert with only some dates and water.

"Why are you doing this?" Hajar (Hagar) asked.

"Because Allah wishes me to," replied Ibrahim (Abraham).

Soon afterward, the water ran out, and there was nowhere to shelter from the baking heat. Hajar (Hagar) and Isma'il (Ishmael) were very thirsty. But where could Hajar (Hagar) find water in the desert? Everywhere she looked was dusty and dry. Perhaps there would be water in the nearby hills? So Hajar (Hagar) left Isma'il (Ishmael) behind and walked from one hill to the other, back and forth, back and forth, but she couldn't find any water.

Whatever would they do?

Then she heard a voice calling to her, and she saw the angel, Jibril (Gabriel), standing

Did you know?

On Hajj, pilgrims remember Hajra's (Hagar's) story. After visiting the Ka'bah, they go to drink from the ancient well of Zamzam. Then they follow Hajar's (Hagar's) path between the two hills of Al-Safa and Al-Marwa. But they do not have to walk through the baking desert as Hajar (Hagar) did. A long, modern building runs between the two hills. Pilgrims can walk up and down, or if they have a medical condition, they can be pushed in wheelchairs.

close by. The angel was pointing at Isma'il (Ishmael).

Suddenly, Hajar (Hagar) saw water gushing up out of the earth around Isma'il's (Ishmael's) feet. There was water she and Isma'il (Ishmael) could drink. Allah had provided for them. This spring became known as Zamzam and its fame spread far and wide.

The Prophet Migrates to Madinah (Medina)

For many years, the Prophet Muhammad lived in Makkah (Mecca), the city of his birth. Here he began to teach people to follow the word of Allah and to accept Islam. At first, he taught only his friends and family, but many people came to hear him and listened carefully to what he said. Many followed him and became Muslims. But some people in Makkah (Mecca) did not like his message. The rich merchants were afraid of losing their power if people began to follow Allah. They offered him bribes to stop his preaching, but Muhammad would not give up. Allah told Muhammad to leave for the city of Madinah (Medina), where he and his followers would be safe.

But the rich merchants of Makkah (Mecca) were secretly plotting to kill Muhammad before he could leave.

"We'll kill him early in the morning when he leaves his house to go to pray," they said.

But the angel Jibril (Gabriel) appeared to Muhammad in his sleep and warned him of their wicked plot. The Prophet asked his cousin, Ali, to sleep in his house instead of him with Muhammad's cloak over him. He promised that Ali would come to no harm.

Then Muhammad and his friend Abu Bakr made their getaway. They climbed on the backs of two swift camels and set off across the desert to Madinah (Medina). When the merchants found out that they had been tricked, they were furious. They offered a reward of 100 camels to anyone who would bring them back. Then, they and their men set off after them.

The Prophet and Abu Bakr tried once again to fool their enemies, by riding south instead of north. But still they were followed. All night they rode on through the desert. Then, when day dawned, they found a cool mountain cave to shelter from the heat. Hot on their heels came the merchants and their men.

"Whatever shall we do?" asked Abu Bakr. "They're getting closer and are sure to see the entrance of the cave."

"Allah will protect us," Muhammad calmly replied.

And this is what happened. The men drew closer and closer, until they stood at the entrance of the cave. Muhammad and Abu Bakr could clearly hear their voices.

"Look!" one voice said. "A cave. They must be in there."

"Don't be silly," another voice said. "No one's entered this cave for years. It's got a huge spider's web right across the entrance, and there's a dove sitting on its nest. No one's been near here, that's for sure."

Then the men went away. When at last Abu Bakr was sure they had gone, he turned to the Prophet.

"Where did the dove and the spider's web come from?" he asked. "They weren't here when we came in."

The Prophet smiled. Allah had protected them, as he knew Allah would.

A few days later, when at last it was safe to leave the cave, they continued their desert journey to Madinah (Medina) where they received a very warm welcome. When they reached the city, Muhammad's camel stopped by a place where the dates were laid out to dry, and here the Prophet built the first mosque.

Did you know?

Muhammad's journey from Makkah (Mecca) to Madinah (Medina) is known as the *hijrah*, or "migration." It took place in the year 622. This date marks the start of the Islamic calendar. The letters AH are written after Muslim years to mean "the year of the hijrah." The Prophet died in Madinah (Medina) in 632.

Did you know?

Today, there are more than 1 billion Muslims all over the world. Islam is the fastest-growing religion. Most Muslims live in the Middle East, Asia, and Africa, in countries where Islam is the official religion. Although all Muslims share the same basic beliefs, there are several different groups. The largest groups are called the Sunni and the Shi'a. The worldwide family of Muslims is called the Ummah, or community.

Glossary

Abu Bakr—close friend of Muhammad who accompanied him on his migration from Makkah (Mecca) to Madinah (Medina)

Allah—the Arabic name for God

angels—heavenly beings created from light and carrying the commands of God in the universe

biography—an account of a person's life story

Dome of the Rock—a mosque in Jerusalem; inside is the sacred rock from which Muslims believe that Muhammad made his Night Journey

five pillars—five duties which Muslims follow in their lives

Hadith—books (or collections) of sayings and actions of the Prophet Muhammad; Muslims use them as guides in their own lives

Hajj—the pilgrimage to Makkah (Mecca) that all Muslims try to make at least once in their lives

hijrah—the name Muslims give to Muhammad's flight from Makkah (Mecca) to Madinah (Medina); word "hijrah" means "migration"

Ibrahim (Abraham)—a great prophet of Islam known as the Friend of Allah

Id-ul-Adha—the festival at the end of the hajj when Muslims remember how Ibrahim (Abraham) almost sacrificed his son for Allah

Id-ul-Fitr—the festival when Muslims celebrate the end of fasting during Ramadan

Islam—the religion of the Muslims who believe in one God, called Allah, and follow his guidance in their lives

Jerusalem—a holy city from which Muhammad made his Night Journey

Jibril (Gabriel)—the angel sent by Allah to tell Muhammad the words of the holy Qur'an

Ka'bah—a cube-shaped shrine in Makkah (Mecca); Muslims always turn to face the Ka'bah when they pray

Khadijah—Muhammad's wife

Madinah (Medina)—a city in Saudi Arabia to which Muhammad migrated to in 622; he died here in 632; a holy city for Muslims

Makkah (Mecca)—a city in Saudi Arabia where Muhammad was born; the Muslims' holiest city

miracles—amazing and supernatural events that cannot be explained

mosque—a building where Muslims meet and pray; also known as Masjid

Muhammad—the last and one of the greatest prophets of Islam; Muslims believe that he was sent by Allah to teach people how to live; received the words of the holy Qur'an from the angel Jibril (Gabriel)

Musa (Moses)—a great prophet of Islam

Muslims—people who follow the religion of Islam and who submit to the will of Allah

Paradise—the name used by Muslims for heaven

pbuh—Muslims write these letters after the prophets' names; short for "peace be upon him"

pilgrimage—special journey to a holy place

prophet—someone chosen by Allah to speak to people about his wishes for the world

Qur'an—the Muslims' holy book

Ramadan—a month during which Muslims fast (do not eat or drink) between dawn and sunset each day

Saudi Arabia—a country in the Middle East where Muhammad lived and where Islam began

Index

To Learn More

At the Library

Bowker, John Westerdale. *World Religions.* New York: DK Publishing, 2003.

Dounda, Kelly. *Religions Around the World.* Edina, Minn.: Abdo Publishing, 2004.

Osborne, Mary Pope. *One World, Many Religions: The Way We Worship.* New York: Knopf, 1996.

On the Web

FactHound offers a safe, fun way to find Internet sites related to this book. All of the sites on FactHound have been researched by our staff.

1. Visit *www.facthound.com*
2. Type in this special code for age-appropriate sites: 1404813136
3. Click on the FETCH IT button.

Your trusty FactHound will fetch the best sites for you!

Look for the other books in the Traditional Religious Tales series:

BUDDHIST STORIES
1-4048-1311-X

CHRISTIAN STORIES
1-4048-1312-8

HINDU STORIES
1-4048-1309-8

JEWISH STORIES
1-4048-1310-1

SIKH STORIES
1-4048-1314-4